P9-BZF-515

CAN WE SHARE THE WORLD WITH TIGERS?

Robert E. Wells

Albert Whitman & Company, Chicago, Illinois

**For my son Jeff, my granddaughters Hope and Hannah,
and to the memory of my daughter-in-law Janeen.**

Library of Congress Cataloging-in-Publication Data

Wells, Robert E.
Can we share the world with tigers? / by Robert E. Wells.
p. cm.
ISBN 978-0-8075-1055-1 (hardcover)
1. Bengal tiger—India—Juvenile literature. 2. Bengal tiger—Conservation—
India—Juvenile literature. 3. Wildlife conservation—India—Juvenile literature.
4. Endangered species—India—Juvenile literature. I. Title.
QL737.C23W433 2012   599.7560954—dc23   2011038269

Text and illustrations copyright © 2012 by Robert E. Wells.
Published in 2012 by Albert Whitman & Company.
Printed in China.
10 9 8 7 6 5 4 3 2 1 BP 16 15 14 13 12

The illustration media are pen and acrylic.
The design is by Carol Gildar and Robert E. Wells.

For more information about Albert Whitman & Company,
please visit our web site at www.albertwhitman.com.

Also by Robert E. Wells:

Can You Count to a Googol?

Did a Dinosaur Drink This Water?

How Do You Know What Time It Is?

How Do You Lift a Lion?

Is a Blue Whale the Biggest Thing There Is?

Polar Bear, Why Is Your World Melting?

What's Faster Than a Speeding Cheetah?

What's Older Than a Giant Tortoise?

What's Smaller Than a Pygmy Shrew?

What's So Special About Planet Earth?

Why Do Elephants Need the Sun?

Bengal tigers live in the forests and grasslands of India. But there are not many left. They are in danger of becoming extinct.

This female tiger, or tigress, and her cubs are heading toward a favorite watering hole.

Suddenly, a warning screech from a langur monkey stops them in their tracks.

Danger is ahead, hidden in the grass on the path.

It's a trap set by a poacher—a hunter who illegally traps wild animals for profit.

SPRING-LOADED TIGER TRAP

TIGER'S PAW
ACTIVATES
TRIGGER,

TRAPPING
TIGER'S LEG

Thousands of tigers have been killed by poachers. This tigress is grateful she wasn't one of them!

Poaching is one reason tigers are in danger.

You'll see an even greater threat at the edge of the forest . . .

Farmers and ranchers are cutting down forest trees and plowing up grassland, taking away the tigers' NATURAL HABITATS for their crops and livestock.

Tigers are predators, which means they hunt other animals—their prey—for food.
The tigers' prey depend on the same habitat for their food.

If the habitat is destroyed, then the tigers' prey will starve—and the tigers will starve too.

People require land for their needs, just as tigers do.

But more than 90 percent of the Bengal tigers' original habitats have been taken over by farmers and ranchers!

ORGANIZATIONS AROUND THE WORLD ARE WORKING TO SAVE TIGERS.

They help protect tigers from poachers and assist farmers in finding other land to grow food and raise cattle.

Although still endangered, India's tiger population has increased slightly in recent years—

bringing new hope to tigers everywhere!

But other habitats around the world are also being disrupted, threatening many other plants and animals.

Some coal and iron mines destroy mountaintops and hillsides,

killing plants and wildlife.

Factories can pollute water, killing fish, frogs, birds, and vegetation.

Is it possible for us to live in harmony with Earth's other living things?

Many thousands of years ago, there were fewer people, and habitat destruction was not widespread.

People lived by hunting and gathering,

which caused little change to natural habitats.

About 10,000 years ago, farming and raising animals began to replace hunting and gathering.

In order to farm and live in villages, people made lots of changes to their habitats.

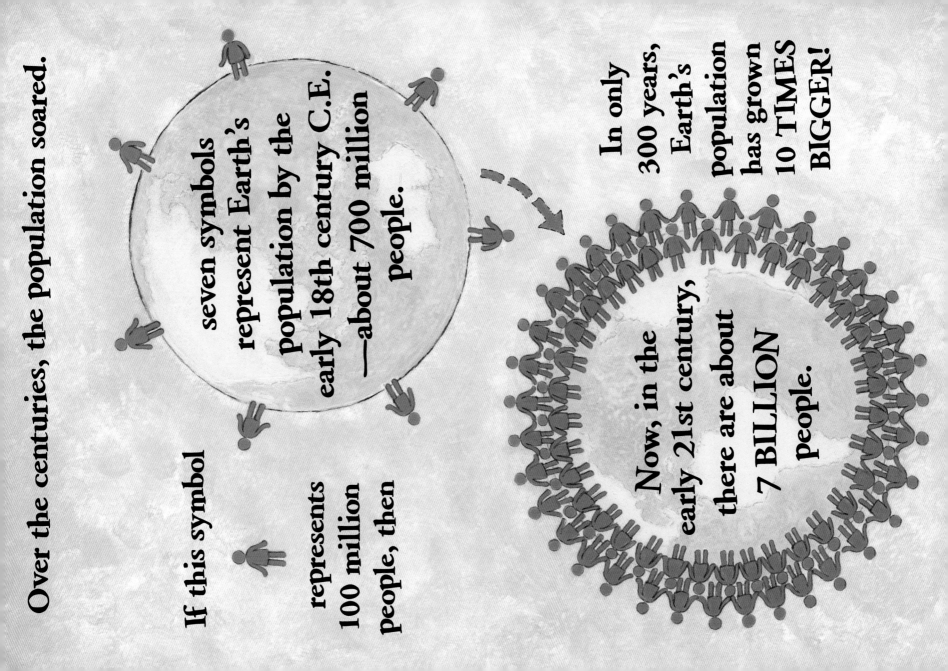

Over the centuries, the population soared.

seven symbols represent Earth's population by the early 18th century C.E. —about 700 million people.

If this symbol represents 100 million people, then

In only 300 years, Earth's population has grown 10 TIMES BIGGER!

Now, in the early 21st century, there are about 7 BILLION people.

Those billions of people continue to change Earth's habitats to suit their needs.

Now there are cities, towns, and villages all over the world!

More than half of the world's people live in cities.

Because there are so many of us, this is probably a good thing . . .

On average, a city dweller uses less land than a person living in a town or village.

Even so, the population keeps growing, so cities, towns, villages, and farms keep spreading out.

As people take up more land, natural habitats are destroyed, endangering thousands of species of living things.

PEOPLE DISRUPT NATURAL HABITATS IN OTHER WAYS, TOO.

We heat buildings and power machines with fossil fuels such as coal and oil. Fossil fuels emit carbon dioxide, or CO_2, which stores the sun's heat.

We need some CO_2 in the air to keep Earth comfortably warm. But too much CO_2 is being released into the air, changing the climate in many habitats.

Because Arctic air is warmer now, summer ice melts faster in the Arctic Ocean,

reducing polar bears' ability to hunt.

Other air pollutants can also cause great harm. Costa Rica's golden toad has recently become extinct, along with 20 other species of frogs and toads.

The likely causes were airborne pesticides, and warmer, drier air that helped spread disease.

EXTRA CO$_2$ IN THE AIR ALSO CHANGES OCEAN HABITATS.

Warmer air warms the ocean, threatening sea life that is sensitive to temperature shifts.

Plus, seawater absorbs the extra CO$_2$, changing the water's chemical balance

and making it difficult for corals to form the hard shells they need.

This endangers the thousands of sea creatures that depend on coral reefs for protection.

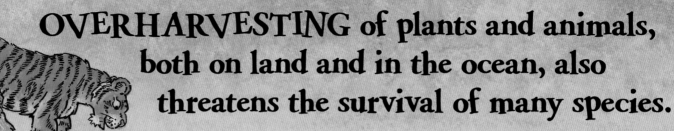

OVERHARVESTING of plants and animals, both on land and in the ocean, also threatens the survival of many species.

For example, excessive commercial fishing has reduced the numbers of many kinds of fish—

such as Atlantic cod and bluefin tuna—

to dangerously low levels.

Sometimes people transport plants or animals from one habitat to another, upsetting the new habitat's natural balance. That plant or animal is called an INVASIVE SPECIES.

In the 1850s, 24 European rabbits were brought to Australia's wilderness for the purpose of hunting.

They soon multiplied into the MILLIONS, eating and destroying many native plant species.

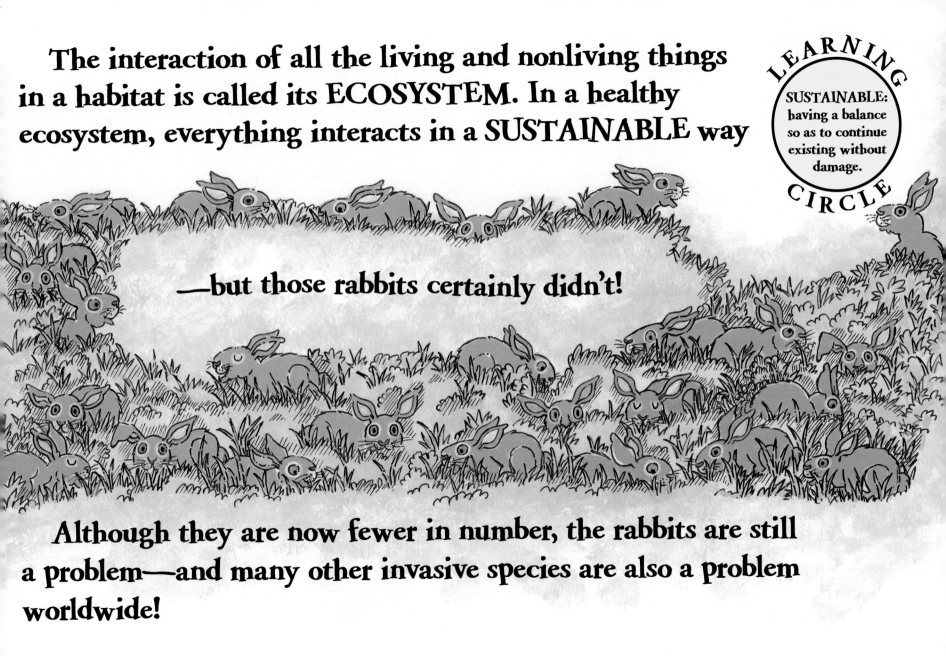

The interaction of all the living and nonliving things in a habitat is called its ECOSYSTEM. In a healthy ecosystem, everything interacts in a SUSTAINABLE way

—but those rabbits certainly didn't!

Although they are now fewer in number, the rabbits are still a problem—and many other invasive species are also a problem worldwide!

EARTH'S HABITATS ARE HOME TO MILLIONS OF SPECIES!

These millions of species— along with people— are all part of Earth's BIODIVERSITY: the variety of living things.

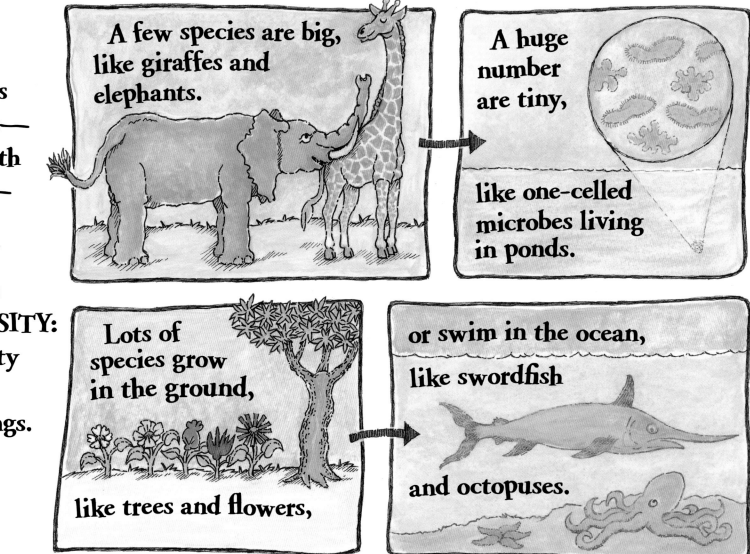

A few species are big, like giraffes and elephants.

A huge number are tiny, like one-celled microbes living in ponds.

Lots of species grow in the ground, like trees and flowers,

or swim in the ocean, like swordfish and octopuses.

Some run fast, like cheetahs and ostriches,

or move slowly, like turtles and snails.

Many fly in the air, like robins or eagles.

A tremendous number are insects and spiders!

Biodiversity helps keep ecosystems healthy and sustainable. But somewhere in the world, a species goes extinct, on average, every 20 MINUTES!

200 MYA
150 MYA
100 MYA
50 MYA
NOW

4th MASS EXTINCTION

AGE OF DINOSAURS

5th MASS EXTINCTION

AGE OF MAMMALS

A mass extinction occurs when at least half of all species go extinct during a short time: perhaps 1,000 years.

Compared to Earth's age, 1,000 years is like a blink of an eye!

The last of the dinosaurs became extinct during the 5th mass extinction.

It was probably caused by an asteroid that devastated the dinosaurs' habitats.

LEARNING CIRCLE

Volcanic eruptions, along with natural changes in climate, may have caused the first four mass extinctions.

Because of habitat loss, climate change, overharvesting, and invasive species, the extinction rate now is as great as it was when the last dinosaurs died out.

5th MASS EXTINCTION

AGE OF MAMMALS

100 MYA

50 MYA

NOW

Scientists fear we may be heading toward a 6th mass extinction— if we don't do something about it!

FORTUNATELY, THERE IS STILL PLENTY OF BIODIVERSITY REMAINING ON EARTH. HOW CAN WE SAVE WHAT'S LEFT?

Many scientists believe we should focus conservation efforts on habitats with the greatest biodiversity, such as rainforests and coral reefs.

They are known as
HOT SPOTS of biodiversity.

LEARNING

Scientists believe rainforests contain millions of undiscovered species!

CIRCLE

Of course, we should also work to save species in other habitats. Every species is important!

Earth's variety of living things work together to help keep our water safe to drink and to protect our food sources.

A newly discovered plant might be used to create a new medicine for a now-incurable disease.

When a species goes extinct, it is gone forever. We'd never know how valuable an undiscovered one might have been!

Here's a whole stack of things people can do to help make Earth balanced and sustainable.

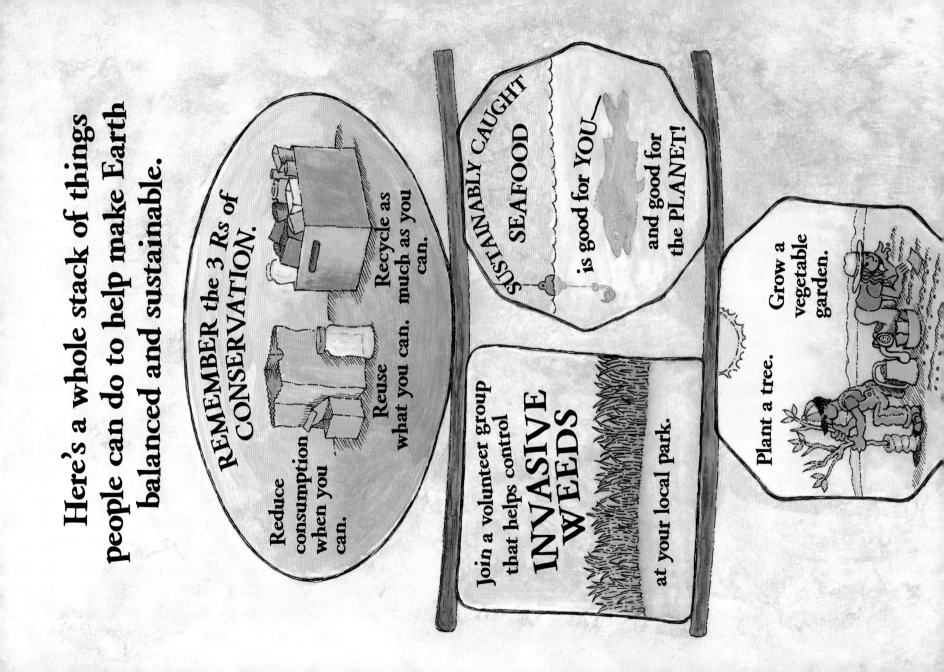

REMEMBER the 3 Rs of CONSERVATION.

Reduce consumption when you can.

Reuse what you can.

Recycle as much as you can.

SUSTAINABLY CAUGHT SEAFOOD

is good for YOU—

and good for the PLANET!

Join a volunteer group that helps control INVASIVE WEEDS at your local park.

Plant a tree.

Grow a vegetable garden.

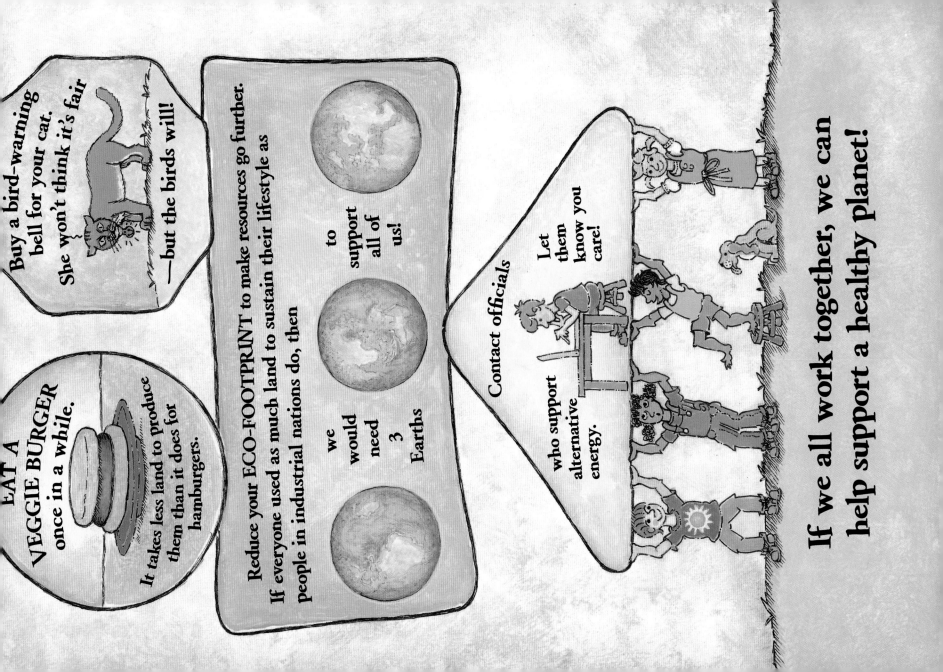

EAT A VEGGIE BURGER once in a while.

It takes less land to produce them than it does for hamburgers.

Buy a bird-warning bell for your cat. She won't think it's fair —but the birds will!

Reduce your ECO-FOOTPRINT to make resources go further. If everyone used as much land to sustain their lifestyle as people in industrial nations do, then

we would need 3 Earths

to support all of us!

Contact officials who support alternative energy. Let them know you care!

If we all work together, we can help support a healthy planet!

THE WORLD IS A MIGHTY BIG PLACE.

But people are taking up so much of the room.

Can we learn better ways of sharing space with all the other creatures living on Earth?

Can we leave some room for tigers?

Glossary

ALTERNATIVE ENERGY: renewable energy that comes from sources other than fossil fuels, such as solar or wind power

BIODIVERSITY: the great variety of living things on Earth that interact and support one another in their natural habitats

ECO-FOOTPRINT: the amount of Earth's nonrenewable resources and energy that individuals use in their everyday lives

ECOSYSTEM: the interactions of all the living and nonliving things in a habitat

EXTINCT SPECIES: a species that once existed on Earth, but no longer does

FOSSIL FUELS: fuels, such as oil, coal, or natural gas, that have been preserved deep under Earth's surface for millions of years

HOT SPOTS OF BIODIVERSITY: habitats designated by scientists that have an exceptionally large number of species interacting with one another

INVASIVE SPECIES: a species that has been transported from one habitat to another and that interferes with the balance in its new habitat

MASS EXTINCTION: when a large number of species become extinct in a short geological period of time

MICROBES: one-celled organisms that are usually microscopic, or not visible to the unaided eye

NATURAL HABITATS: areas where particular plants and animals usually live

OVERHARVESTING: taking away more animals or plants from their natural habitats than can be replaced by natural processes

SPECIES: a particular kind of plant or animal that usually has the ability to produce like offspring

SUSTAINABLE: having a balance so as to continue existing without damage